Wonders
of the
North Pole

British Library Cataloguing in Publication Data
A catalogue record is available from the British Library

ISBN: 0-8109-1431-X
ISBN 13: 978-0-8109-1431-X

Copyright © Éditions de la Martinière, France
English translation copyright © Éditions de la Martinière, France

Layout for English version: Christophe Tardieux

Printed and bound in Belgium
10 9 8 7 6 5 4 3 2 1

HNA
harry n. abrams, inc.
a subsidiary of La Martinière Groupe

Wonders
of the
North Pole

Photographs by Francis Latreille

Texts by
Catherine Guigon

Illustrations by
Frédéric Malenfer

ABRAMS BOOKS FOR YOUNG READERS
NEW YORK

CONTENTS

How these images came to you…

It is no easy matter exploring the frozen regions of the Arctic Circle and the North Pole. Your fingers go numb in the cold. Blizzards try to tear the camera from your hands. But Francis has fallen in love with the changing light of the Arctic and thinks a Polar expedition is a real treat!

The beauty of a frozen landscape was first revealed to Francis when he was six; the winter in the Loire valley was savage and the thermometer went down to −20° Celsius. One morning, he saw white 'pancakes' spreading over the river's surface: ice was forming. When the ice had solidified, he was wrapped up warmly and sent out to skate on the river. This was his first experience of venturing out onto the ice and the memory has never left him.

Years later, when he was already a famous photographer, Francis had the chance to accompany the famous explorer and doctor, Jean-Louis Étienne, on a mission to the North Pole. It was something of an ordeal. His feet slipped on the powdery snow and his fingers froze. But his love for icy landscapes prevailed. Now he adores the magical light of the tundra, the frozen waste of the north, and the Northern Lights.

The Arctic is one of the last wild places left on the planet. There are no roads or railways there. Wherever he goes, Francis uses the local means of transport: snowmobiles or sleighs drawn by dogs or reindeer. Long distances are covered by helicopter or boat—and sometimes the boat is an icebreaker.

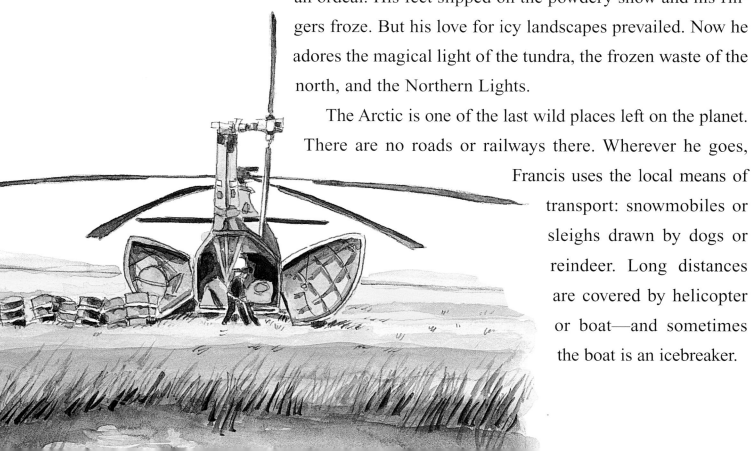

To survive on your own in the polar region is quite an adventure. You need a lot of equipment. Francis sleeps under canvas in a top-quality sleeping bag made from the down (inner feathers) of geese or eider ducks. (That's right: eiderdown!) He dresses in lots of thin, warm layers: cotton on the inside, wool and fleece next, then wind-proofs. But the most important thing is not to run out of kerosene. All the water in the Arctic is frozen and has to be melted for drinking. Moreover, you need hot food and most of your food is dehydrated, freeze-dried or in powder, so you need water to make it up. You have to carry about a kilo of food per person per day. Cameras too are sensitive to the cold; below –25° Celsius, film becomes very brittle and batteries quickly run down. And you must be careful to avoid sudden changes of temperature: when you come into a heated room, condensation may form in the camera lens and damage it.

The polar regions also have one or two surprises in store—like the day Francis found himself face to face with a polar bear! He had to beat a hasty retreat, dumping his equipment. Fortunately, his pilot spotted the danger and set the helicopter-blades revolving to frighten the bear off. Francis was saved but it was quite a fright! Unlike the polar bears, the people who live in the Arctic region are very friendly. If you want to communicate, be patient, thoughtful and smile a lot!

The lands around the North Pole

The climate around the North Pole

The climate around the North Pole is polar, that is, very, very cold. In winter the average temperature is −25° Celsius and in summer 10° Celsius is about the maximum. The air is dry because the Arctic Ocean is under a bank of ice most of the time and does not evaporate.
Different kinds of ice form:
– The ice-shelf or sea ice. This is saline because it is made of sea-water, which freezes at −1.8° Celsius.
– Glacier ice, made of packed snow and therefore of fresh water. These glaciers constitute the icecap or *inlandsis*, which covers most of Greenland apart from its coasts. Where these glaciers meet the coast, they produce icebergs: great blocks of frozen freshwater that have broken off to float away in the sea.

The People

In the past, the natives of the polar regions were nomadic hunters, who had adapted to the extreme living conditions. Today, most of them have settled for life in one place and have access to modern comfort. These include: the Inuits of the Canadian Far North and Greenland (150,000); the Sámi of Scandinavia and Russia (70,000) and, among the many Siberian peoples, the Dolgans (7,000). Only a third of the Sámi and some 250 Dolgans still live the nomadic life, shepherding their herds of reindeer.

Animal life (Fauna)

Despite the harsh climate, many mammals live in the Polar Circle, including some 25,000 polar bears, many of them in Canada. Canada also boasts wolves, arctic foxes and small rodents called lemmings. The Siberian tundra is home to large herds of reindeer, many of them tame. In summer, migrant birds nest in the Far North. And finally, the waters of the Arctic Ocean are rich in fish, particularly caplin and cod, which are hunted by the colonies of seals and walrus.

Plant life (Flora)

Neither deciduous trees nor conifers can survive in these latitudes. On the permanently frozen subsoil of the tundra, a mixture of mosses, lichens and herbaceous plants turns green in summer and explodes into flower. These flowers are small and tough enough to survive the cold. You also see fungi and edible berries.

The glacial Arctic Ocean is the smallest ocean in the world at 14.8 million square kilometres. The circumpolar regions have an area of around 7.5 million square kilometres.

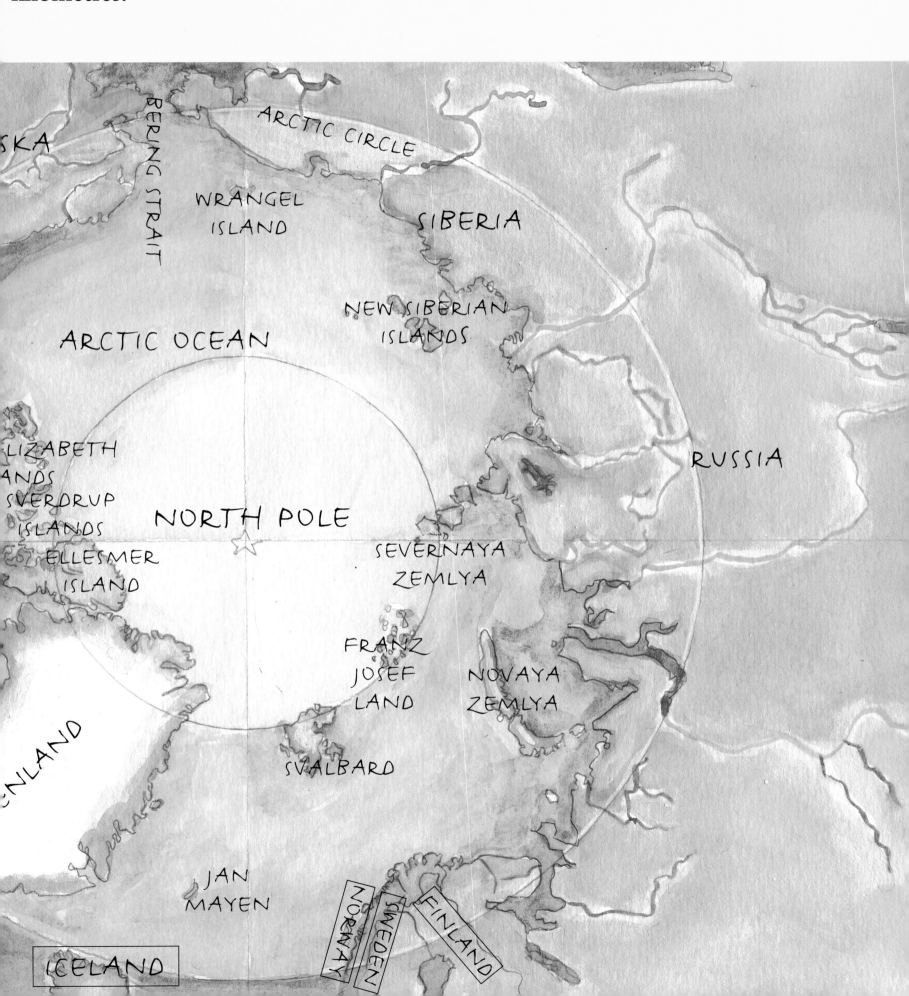

The regions of the Arctic Circle

The Arctic Ocean is partly frozen throughout the year. An ice sheet several metres deep forms on its surface. This sea of ice breaks up into enormous plates under the influence of the ocean currents.

The glacial Arctic Ocean is well-named. Part of its surface, exposed to temperatures as low as –70° Celsius, is permanently frozen. The North Pole, which lies on the latitude of 90°N is in the middle of the sea. It is a 'virtual' geographical point used as a reference-point in mapping the earth.

Moving outwards from the North Pole toward the Polar Circle (the line beyond which the sun never rises in winter), we see land rising from the sea. These lands encircling the Arctic Ocean are called the circumpolar regions (regions around the Pole) and amount to a total of 7.5 million square kilometres. Most of this is composed of Alaska, the Canadian Far North, Scandinavian Lapland and Siberia. To this we must add Greenland, the largest island in the world (2.166 million square kilometres) and other smaller islands like the Queen Elizabeth Islands and the Novaya Zemlya and Spitzbergen archipelagos (groups of islands).

These regions have certain things in common. Because they are so close to the Pole, their winter is one long polar night and their summer one long polar day. Vegetation is rare because of the cold. The only things that grow there are mosses, lichens and some herbaceous plants.

The lands around the North Pole are a long way from the great capitals.

Sea ice in perpetual motion

Sea ice is not frozen into immobility. Here you see it striated with cracks and channels.

Ice starts forming on the sea at −1.8° Celsius. So a lot of ice forms on the Arctic Ocean! It forms a kind of shell over the sea, made from plates of ice that are constantly moved about by ocean currents and the wind. It is studded with chaotic blocks of ice that scientists call 'pressure ridges'. These occur when several sheets of ice collide and raft over each other or are forced upwards. The ridges can be ten metres high and several kilometres long. But the ice sheet can also be sufficiently smooth and sufficiently thick (3–4 metres) to form a landing strip for an aircraft. Sometimes it cracks and forms 'leads' or channels. Experience and care are needed by those exploring this unstable environment, as the landscape can change quite suddenly.

With the rising temperatures of summer, the ice sheet breaks up into floes and forms pack ice. The surface area of the sea ice varies with the seasons: in winter, it covers almost the entire Arctic Ocean whereas, in summer, it covers only about 5 million square kilometres.

In summer, it is possible to use a kayak to move through the ice floes.

Breaking the ice sheet

Propelled by powerful motors, the icebreaker opens its own road through the thickest ice sheet, which it breaks beneath its own weight.

In the past, ships kept away from the Arctic Ocean in winter, when there was a danger of their vessel being trapped and crushed by the ice floes. Many sailors lost their lives when their ships were wrecked in this way.

Icebreakers came into use early in the twentieth century to avert this danger. They are of very special design. The hull (the sloping sides of the ship) is reinforced with something like steel armour; the prow (front) of the ship is rounded to allow it slide up over the ice and crush it; and the motors are very powerful so that the ship can move forward through the thickest ice.

One of the Arctic territories, Russia, has developed especially powerful icebreakers to allow ships to use its northern ports. The *Yamal* has nuclear motors yielding 75,000 horsepower; they allow it to take on ice floes several metres thick. These icebreakers transport food and equipment, and thanks to them, the Siberian coast is no longer so isolated during the long winter night. But the best way of getting around is by helicopter. Regular helicopter flights all around the frozen north are interrupted only by very bad weather. They bring the post and supplies and can take the severely ill to hospital.

There are no roads through the Russian tundra. Helicopters become 'flying lorries'.

The people of the Arctic Circle

The immense territories of the Arctic region are inhabited by peoples native to it. They include the Inuits, the Sámi, the Dolgans and other Siberian peoples.

The Arctic peoples belong to a number of different countries. They used to wander with their herds, a way of life called nomadic. But now they have mostly settled in one place. They live in villages and towns, though many often return to the ice sheet to renew their traditional way of life.

The Inuits (around 150,000 of them) live in Alaska, which is one of the United States of America, in Canada (particularly in Nunavut) and in Greenland (an autonomous province of Denmark). They used to be called 'Eskimos' by their enemies, the Native Americans of Canada, and later by Westerners. But it is an insulting name, which means 'eaters of raw meat'. Today they prefer to be called 'Inuit', which simply means 'people'. All young Inuits study English or Danish at school. But at home they speak Inuktitut, the Inuit language, whose alphabet has been modernised in order to make it computer-friendly.

The Sámi (formerly called Lapps) are native to Scandinavia. They are thought to number around 70,000 and live in the north of Norway, Sweden, Finland and the Kola Peninsula in Russia. At school and at home, they speak one of the variants of Sámi, a Finno-Ungaric language.

Finally, among the twenty-six ethnic groups found in Siberia, there are some 7,000 Dolgans living in the Taymyr Peninsula (Russia), though only 250 of them are still nomads. They speak Russian and Yakut.

When Inuit children play 'cat's cradle', they represent animals like the fox or the caribou with its antlers.

Migrating east

These photos date from the 1930s, when the French explorer Paul-Émile Victor was studying the 'Eskimos' of Greenland. At the time, almost nothing was known about their history and origins.

The ethnologist and explorer Paul-Émile Victor (1907–95) devoted part of his life to studying the Inuits of Greenland, who were at the time known as 'Eskimos'. In 1934, he landed on the east shore of the island, at Ammasslik, where he overwintered with the Inuits.

At this time, scientists were astonished by the presence on Greenland of the Inuits, who have Asian features. Today, it is thought that the first Inuits came from Mongolia, which lies between Russia and China. Travelling east, they probably crossed the Bering Strait from Russia to Alaska, where they first settled. Their presence there is confirmed by archaeological remains dating back to 10,000 before our current era. Hounded by the local Native Americans, they are thought to have continued their migration across the Canadian Far North to settle in Greenland between 2050 and 1,700 before our current era. Since then, they have confirmed their ability to survive extremes of temperature and created what Victor called the 'civilisation of the seal': seals provide them with meat to eat, oil for lamps and fur for clothing.

In the past, Inuit children travelled on their mother's back in the hood of her garment.

Seals populate the ice shelf

Seals like to lie out on the ice—in touchingly clumsy poses! But to find their food, these excellent swimmers must dive under the ice.

The seal belongs to the pinniped family and is a perfect example of a marine mammal. It is designed for swimming: its paddle-shaped tail lets it drive swiftly through the water; its ears are nothing more than a hole that the water cannot penetrate; its eyes are adapted for underwater vision; and its nostrils are closed by valves. Consequently it can stay underwater for a long while—between forty-five minutes and two hours. During this time, it stuffs itself with fish, prawns and crabs, before returning to the surface via a hole in the ice. There, of course, it runs the danger of being spotted by a hungry polar bear.

Six different species of seal live in the Far North, each with its own rhythm of life. The Harp seal (4.8 million individuals) makes an annual migration of 3,200 kilometres between the Arctic Ocean, its summer residence, and the Atlantic, where it spends the winters. In March and April, other common seal species, the Bearded, Ringed and Hooded seals, give birth to their young (called 'pups'). The pups suckle for between a few days and a month. The giant of the Arctic pinnipeds is the walrus, which boasts long ivory tusks. Alas, hunted by the Inuits for its meat and fat, it is on the brink of extinction. A few colonies of walrus survive in Greenland and Siberia.

The Inuit harpoon is terribly effective, even against the walrus, which can weigh up to a ton.

The discovery of the Arctic

Venturing into the Arctic regions, sailors and explorers braved great danger. Even today, a boat can be trapped by the shifting ice.

Explorers discovered the northern regions very early in the history of humanity. The earliest known explorer was a Greek, Pytheas the Massaliot, who left Marseille aboard his oared galley. In 330 before our current era, he reached the 'land of Thule', supposedly the Faroe Islands. Later, in 982, a Viking called Erik the Red 'discovered' Greenland.

From the sixteenth century on, navigators tried to locate or open a passage through the ice. Some sought the 'North-Eastern Passage' along the Siberian coast; others sought the 'North-Western Passage' along the North American coast. Such a passage would make it easier to trade with people on the other side of the world. And many died in the attempt, among them the Dutchman Willem Barents, who discovered Spitzbergen in 1597; the Englishman Henry Hudson, who came within 1,065 kilometres of the North Pole in 1607; and the Dane, Vitus Bering, who died in 1741 having crossed the strait between the American and Asian continents and given his name to it—the Bering Strait.

Between 1893 and 1896 the Norwegian Fridtjof Nansen finally discovered the existence of the glacial Arctic Ocean. For three years, he let his ship the *Fram* drift before the ocean currents. On his return to Norway, he was greeted as a hero.

Pack ice is still a danger to ships and can sometimes trap the unsuspecting.

The conquest of the North Pole

The Pole is simply a geographical point on the ice sheet at 90° North. But the difficulty of attaining it made it an obsession with nineteenth-century explorers.

In the early twentieth century every explorer dreamed of reaching the mythical North Pole. One such man, Robert Edwin Peary, was determined to be the first to do so. He had already tried seven times!

On March 1, 1909, Peary had reached the latitude of 87° 47' North. He was only 200 kilometres from the Pole. He prepared his sleighs for the final approach across the ice. Four Inuits and his faithful servant Matthew Henson accompanied him. On April 6, 1909, his dream seemed to have come true: he had reached the North Pole. But when he returned to civilisation, a terrible disappointment awaited him. The newspapers, which he had not read during his expedition, were full of the exploits of another American, Frederick Cook, who claimed to have reached the Pole on April 21 of the previous year. A fierce argument broke out between the two men. Eventually, the experts decided in Peary's favour and he was declared the first man to reach the North Pole. Today, some wonder whether Peary would have had enough time between March and April 1900 to reach the Pole and return. After all, that would have meant an exhausting 400 kilometre return trip over the ice.

Many more have since reached the North Pole, but it is always very challenging!

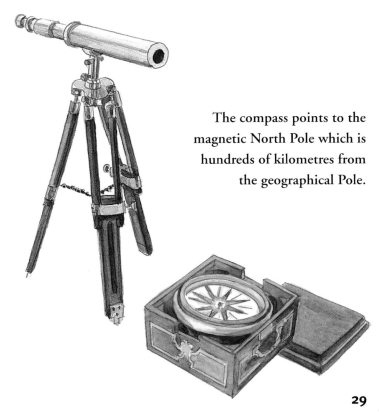

The compass points to the magnetic North Pole which is hundreds of kilometres from the geographical Pole.

Bitter cold

The very low temperatures make the Arctic climate almost unbearable. Blizzards, wind, snow and fog are common. Survival is possible only by protecting oneself from the cold.

The harsh climate of the Arctic is explained by the very few hours of sunlight received there. The sun never rises high enough in the sky to warm the atmosphere. There are two main seasons: winter and summer. In winter, the days are short and the nights very long. The average temperature is –25° Celsius. Winter lasts about six months. During the three months of summer, the nights are very short, the days very long and luminous and the temperatures rarely go higher than 10° Celsius. Between the two, spring and autumn last only a few short weeks each.

The Arctic climate is very dry. Sea water (because it is salty) freezes at –1.8° Celsius and, once frozen, does not evaporate. Without humidity, there are few clouds in the sky and precipitation (water falling as rain or snow) is rare. Less than 250 millimetres of water a year falls in the Arctic Circle. In this, it paradoxically resembles the arid expanses of the Sahara!

These climatic conditions have allowed the formation of glaciers. Successive layers of snow, building up to hundreds of metres in depth, have, over several million years, produced these rivers of ice.

This Dolgan is battling with the cold. His eyes are protected from the very intense sunlight by dark glasses.

The work of the wind

The winds of the polar region are very violent and very dangerous. But they also sculpt the ice into strange and magnificent forms.

Winds can suddenly rise in the Arctic region, instantly conjuring severe weather conditions from a clear, blue sky.

Of all the Arctic winds, the blizzard is the best known. It brings with it squalls of snow that limit visibility and hide every landmark. Sometimes you can barely see your own feet in a blizzard!

Catabatic winds can occur in the Arctic. Air cooled by a glacier flows down the slope of the ice sheet toward the shore, gaining speed as it goes. They can attain very high speeds and have been known to carry away whole buildings!

The most violent winds in the northern hemisphere are found in Greenland, especially in the Amassalik region on the east of the island: peak speeds of 300 kilometres per hour have been recorded.

The strength of the wind intensifies one's sense of cold. This is called the 'wind chill factor' and scientists have made a table of its effects. The 'bite' of the wind is measured in terms of air temperature and the speed of the wind. Thus a blizzard blowing at 64 kilometres per hour with an air temperature of 20° Celsius will produce a sensation of cold on the skin equivalent to a temperature of −49°Celsius.

And it is by 'biting' the ice that the wind sculpts these strange forms and fantastical animals.

The gusting wind raises swirls of snow and creates 'white light'.

Dressing warmly

These Dolgans look very handsome in their
everyday wear made of reindeer hide,
with matching boots and mittens.

Wearing furs is still the best way to protect oneself from the extreme cold. Animal hides are warm, durable and water-proof. Like the other natives of the Arctic, the Dolgans soon learned to tan, cut and sew garments of leather. Among the Dolgan, these tasks are carried out by women.

Every people has its own traditions. The Inuits tend to wear jackets and anoraks of seal-skin, a very supple leather from which they also make mittens and boots. The Dolgans, like the Sámi, use the skin of the reindeer, which wander over the tundra in herds. But all these peoples take great care with their appearance and love embroidery, wooden and metal charms, and beads. In the past, they acquired them by bartering them for furs with the few foreign traders who came this far north. These days the Dolgans buy them in Khatanga, the capital of the Russian province of Taymyr. But what they most prize is white fur, since the colour white is supposed to deter evil spirits; the best thing of all is the fluffy tail of the Arctic fox.

An Inuit family can dress in nothing but furs.
The men wear trousers made of polar bear skin.

His Majesty the Polar Bear

The polar bear is the lord and master of his ice-shelf hunting grounds. Majestic, often solitary, he rules here by virtue of his strength. His only enemy and predator is humankind.

The polar bear is not exactly cuddly! The biggest carnivore on land, the male polar bear can weigh up to 600 kilograms and the female up to 400. When the male stands upright, he is more than two metres tall and could look an elephant in the eye.

The polar bear is a living symbol of the polar regions. Its Latin name is *Ursus maritimus*. This creature is perfectly adapted to the climate: its 'coat' is very warm and a thick layer of fat beneath affords further insulation from the cold. Its big, webbed feet make the polar bear an excellent swimmer.

Most of its time is spent hunting seals on the ice-shelf. Its fine sense of smell allows it to detect a seal up to thirty kilometres away. A single blow of the bear's massive claws dispatches the seal, which is then eaten.

When the ice-shelf melts in the summer, polar bears take refuge on the coast. There is little for them to eat then and they survive on berries, seaweed and fish. This is when the female digs out a den for herself and gives birth to her cubs. A new born cub is little bigger than a kitten.

There are still around 25,000 polar bears in the Arctic. They live mainly in Greenland, on the shore of Hudson Bay (Canada) and on the Norwegian island of Spitzbergen.

This 'tundra buggy' from Churchill, a town in the Canadian Far North, allows people to get quite close to bears.

Hunting with the Inuits

For the Inuits of today, the hunt has lost none of its thrills. They sledge for dozens of kilometres over the ice in the hope of killing a seal or a bear.

The Inuits have always been great hunters. Their way of life has changed but they still have the right to kill bears and seals in their own territories. In early March, when the days start to lengthen, the men prepare their sleigh-harnesses. The sled dogs are huskies, a dog once cross-bred with wolves, and true athletes. Six dogs pull a sleigh; they can cover a hundred kilometres and go without food for two or three days. They drink by lapping up the snow while still on the run. The lead dog, chosen for its strength and intelligence, is a precious guide. It picks its way carefully over the ice-floes.

At this time of year, the ice-shelf is still solid. It will melt only in May, when summer comes. Till then, the Inuit hunting-grounds gain a massive extension!

Seals are hunted for their flesh, oil and fur. They come up for air and sun themselves on the ice, but they are very wary and must be approached very carefully. The Inuit hunters advance behind a little white veil that makes them, from the seal's point of view, invisible.

Sometimes the Inuits come across the fresh tracks of a polar bear. Tracking it down is dangerous but exciting. If they make a kill, the bear-meat will be shared out between all the inhabitants of the village.

The sled-dogs are trained to be tough. They sleep outside even in winter and are fed on dried fish.

The *Inlandis* of Greenland

In the polar regions, the land is covered with snow or ice throughout almost all of the year. The snowy glaciers transform this part of Greenland into a mystical landscape of dazzling beauty.

Early in the Quaternary era, around 4.1 million years ago, the climate was much colder than it is today. Monstrous glaciers that we call *Inlandis* covered a large part of Europe and North America. Most of these have now disappeared, the exceptions being Greenland in the north and the Antarctica in the south.

Greenland's *Inlandis* was formed over more than two million years ago. An enormously thick layer of ice covers most of the island: the 'icecap'. This dome-shaped mass covers 1.7 million square kilometres in volume and represents some nine per cent of the earth's reserves of fresh water.

Dragged downwards by their weight, the glaciers of the icecap move very slowly. As they move they wear down, or erode, the mountains that they cover.

Closer to the coast, glaciers reach fjords, former glacial valleys invaded by the sea. There they break up and melt in the sea. This is the source of the gigantic icebergs that drift out onto the ocean under the influence of winds and currents.

The Inuits mark out paths with stone landmarks, which they call *inuksuk*, meaning 'man-like'.

Cathedrals of ice

These impressive cliffs of ice are true floating islands. The icebergs from the Arctic travel long distances on the open sea before melting away.

Unlike the ice-shelf, which is formed of frozen sea-water, icebergs are made of freshwater. This is because the glaciers from which they come are made of snow not frozen seawater. Icebergs float because ice is lighter than water. The biggest of them rise some seventy metres from the surface of the sea. But only a part of the iceberg is visible; the underwater part represents some seven-eighths of these great objects. The colours on these cathedrals of ice vary with light, covering the whole spectrum of blue.

Some ninety per cent of the big icebergs adrift in the North Atlantic come from the east coast of Greenland, notably from the wonderfully beautiful glacier of Sermeq Kujalleq, which flows into a fjord near the town of Ilulissat. The other ten per cent come from the Arctic islands east of Canada.

Icebergs travel at an average speed of 0.7 km per hour. Their speed depends on the strength of the winds and currents driving them. They sometimes reach New York in the United States, only to melt 4,000 kilometres away from their source. In 1912, the ocean-liner *Titanic* sank after hitting an iceberg near Newfoundland. Today, ships are warned of approaching icebergs by their radar.

In the past, these mountains of ice would suddenly loom out of the fog, leaving the helmsman no time to avoid them.

In the wake of the whale

This humped-back whale has surfaced off the coast of Greenland in order to breathe. It blasts a jet of water into the air before diving back down to the depths with a great sweep of its tail.

Whales belong to the family of Cetacea. They love the polar oceans, which are rich in krill, a Norwegian word that means 'whale food'. The krill is a tiny translucent shrimp, about six centimetres in length, which swims amid quantities of microscopic seaweed. The combination of the two is called plankton. This is the basic food of aquatic animals. And whales do not hold back on their krill-intake!

Whales are among the largest living creatures on the planet. They can be up to thirty metres long and weigh up to 150 tons.

Whales were long hunted for their very fatty flesh, from which oil was extracted. Whales also have a kind of very stiff barrier of hair that filters what comes into their mouth and these 'baleen' hairs were used to make the struts of umbrellas and to stiffen women's corsets. In the nineteenth century, whale-hunting became an industry and flotillas of whalers scoured the seas. Between 1925 and 1975, more than 1.5 million whales were killed. Consequently, around thirty species are now on the verge of extinction.

In 1986, an international agreement ended the massacre for a while. Unfortunately, some countries, notably Japan, do not respect the agreement and continue to hunt whales.

Every year, nine million tourists travel to see whales.

Colour confronts the night

The natives of the Arctic Circle annually experience the long polar night. So they bring as much colour as they can into their daily lives, painting their houses in vivid shades.

The Arctic people used to be nomads. Whole families would move around the ice-shelf as the fortunes of hunting and fishing dictated. Today, they are almost all sedentarised, living in towns and enjoying the comforts of urban life.

In Greenland, the Inuits live in coastal villages where they have access to supplies brought by sea. Their well-heated houses have telephone and internet access. Sometimes, the villagers still get together to eat raw seal-meat after a successful hunt.

Even town-dwelling Inuits tend to spend their holidays hunting. In winter, hunters build a place where they can rest and take shelter from the storms: an igloo. They cut out blocks of compacted snow with a saw and pile them up into a dome shape.

In 1999, the Canadian Inuits obtained (after long years of negotiation with the government) their own self-ruled territory, the Nunavut, meaning 'our land'. It covers 1.9 million square kilometres of north-west Canada. About one fifth of the population (4,500 out of the 26,600 Canadian Inuits) lives in the capital, Iqaluit.

An igloo takes about three hours to build. Well insulated, it helps conserve body-heat and offers necessary protection from the cold.

The Dolgans: nomads of the tundra

In the Taymyr Peninsula (Russia), reindeers are harnessed as horses used to be in Europe. These tame ruminants (animals that chew the cud) pull the tents of nomadic Dolgans across the tundra.

The Dolgans are among the last nomadic herders to shepherd their reindeer all year round over the plains of Taymyr in Siberia. In winter, the reindeer can still find mosses and lichens to eat beneath the snow but every fortnight they and their shepherds must move on in search of new pastures. At each migration, they travel some ten or fifteen kilometres across the frozen tundra before setting up a new camp.

Their tents—they are more like little houses—are called *baloks*; each is pulled along by a team of eight reindeers. Mounted on runners, they slide over the snow like a sled. An entire family (as many as five or seven people) live in these tiny dwellings, which are made of a wood frame covered with reindeer hide and heated by a wood-burning stove equipped with a metal chimney. The Dolgans also cook at this stove. In summer, they use a lighter tent.

This way of life has continued for over two hundred years. But only about 250 Dolgans now persist with this lifestyle, called transhumance. The others prefer the easier life of the city.

The few Dolgans who persist with the nomadic lifestyle live for their reindeer and take very good care of their herds.

The reindeer of the tundra

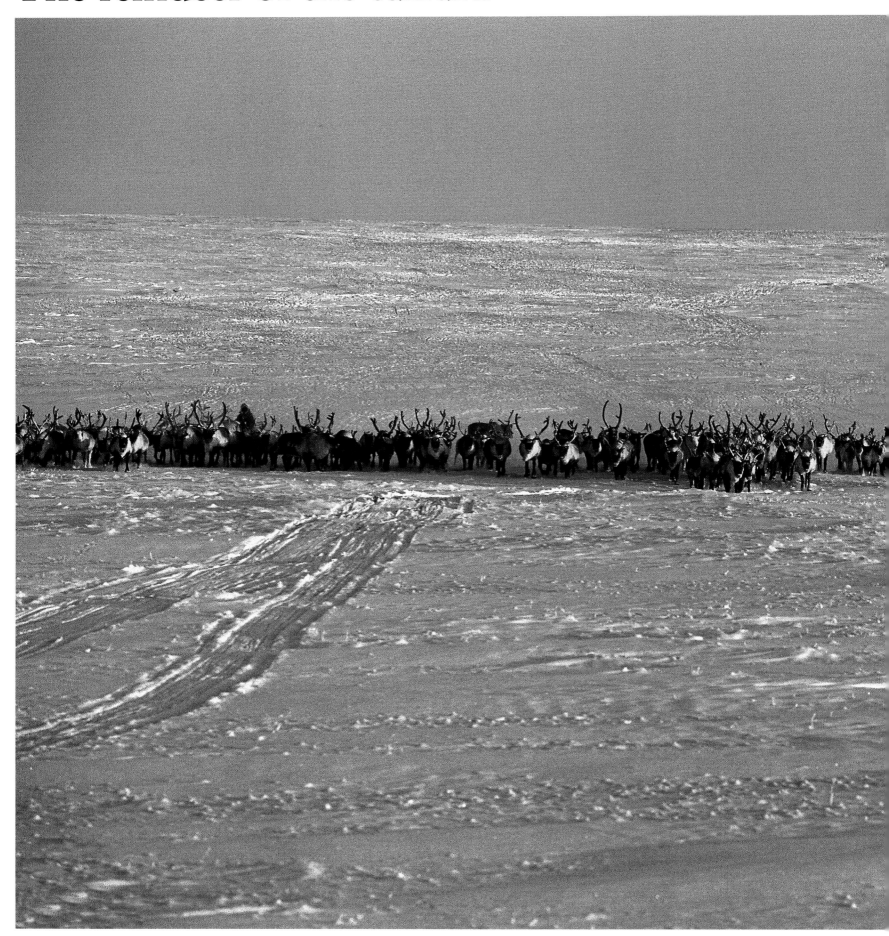

The vast herds of reindeer seek their food under the snow of the Siberian tundra. But this food is scarce, which means that the herds must regularly move on when the food supply is exhausted.

Reindeer, found in northern Europe and Asia, and caribous, found in Northern America, are not identical but are almost certainly the same species. They belong to the family Cervidae and, with their heads crowned by majestic antlers, are the true kings of the tundra. The horns or antlers that grow on their heads are made of bone irrigated by blood vessels. They change colour with the seasons, from red to dark brown, fall off during the winter, and re-grow over the following year. This cumbersome excrescence is a weapon. Male reindeer use it to fight and impose their rule on the herd. In the rutting season, the herd champion acquires a group of females for his own use.

In winter, wild reindeer, which can weigh up to 200 kilograms, find their food under the snow. They scratch with their hooves to expose the buried mosses and lichens. When the snow is frozen solid they can no longer do this and set off on long migrations across the vast frozen plains of Siberia in search of softer snow.

The Sámi and the Siberian tribes have long since domesticated reindeer. They milk them and live off of their meat and milk.

Unlike other Cervidae, both male (stag) and female (doe) reindeer have antlers.

A day in the life of the Dolgans

Fish dry in the winds of the tundra. Their nomadic lifestyle means that Dolgans must provide for almost all their own needs.

Dolgan cattle-breeders live completely independent of others in the tundra. What they need, they must find or make for themselves. Every day, as they shepherd their reindeer-herds, they set traps to catch fur-bearing animals. They generally catch foxes or wolves but sometimes land a bear. Carrying it back to the camp, they cut up the dead animal and eat what they can of it, then tan the hide. The resulting furs are valuable; in the past, they were bartered for other goods but now they are sold in towns. Tradition required that a Dolgan man offer a bear skin to the woman he wanted to marry.

In summer, the Dolgans fish in lakes and rivers. Their catches, gutted and dried in the open air, are eaten by the entire community. In the Taymyr Peninsula, a traditional recipe called *stroganina* is made of fish of the Salmondidae family: the trout, char and salmon of freshwater streams. The fish is stripped of its scales and frozen. Then it is cut up, still frozen, into fine flakes and served with pepper and salt. Tea or vodka (the traditional Russian alcoholic drink) is served with *stroganina*. It takes a little getting used to!

In Canada, the Inuits of Nunavut sculpt and sell objects in a stone called steatite or soapstone.

The polar night

In winter, the sun 'forgets' to rise on the Arctic. It is night almost all the time. But above the Siberian tundra, the Northern Lights cover the sky in narrow bands of colour.

The polar night and its opposite, the 'midnight sun', are explained by the rotation of the earth around the sun. The axis about which the earth rotates is at angle to that of the sun. This is what gives the seasons their rhythm: the shortening of daylight in the winter and the longer days of summer. At the equator, days last twelve hours all year round and do not vary with the season. At the North and South Poles, the shortening and lengthening of daylight is at its most extreme.

Thus, in the northern hemisphere, between 23 September and 31 March the sun does not rise on regions north of the Polar Circle (66.33°N). There are 174 days of almost total darkness at the Pole and ninety days at Thule (Qaanaaq), in Greenland, the world's most northerly town (76°N). Daylight very gradually returns.

One of the most spectacular features of the polar night is the Aurora borealis or the Northern Lights. Long fluorescent veils—green, yellow or blue—undulate in the sky for minutes at a time. These curtains of light were once considered magical. Now we know that they form in the ionosphere, one of the upper layers of the atmosphere, at an altitude of 80 or 150 kilometres. There electrons accelerated by the combined magnetic spheres of the sun and earth collide with atoms of gas; these atoms give off light like the gas in a fluorescent tube.

The Great Bear is particular clear in the Arctic sky. The Ancient Greeks called it *arctos* or 'bear', which is the origin of the world Arctic.

Siberian festivals

Today is a festival in this little Siberian village. They are celebrating the return of the sun after the long polar night. The Dolgans gather to sing and dance before sitting down to a feast.

In late February or early March, the Arctic world celebrates the return of the sun, which begins its slow reconquest of the sky. The days lengthen and the light returns. The date of these festivities varies from country to country but they happen everywhere in the Far North.

In the Taymyr Peninsula, where the Dolgans live, the return of the sun is marked by open-air dancing. Then a great straw man is burnt to symbolise the 'death' of winter. Lasso competitions are organised. The idea is to throw the noose around the legs of a galloping animal and stop it in its tracks. Dolgan men are amazingly good at this.

Evening comes but the festivities go on. For both the Inuits and the Dolgans, the most important traditional instruments are the trumpet and the drum. The drum is shallow and made of taut reindeer hide; it looks like a tambourine and sometimes has little bells attached to it. It beats out the rhythm and supports the choral song. But it is also an instrument of communication with the spirits. Shamans ('witch-doctors') sometimes enter a special mental state, called a trance, when playing it.

For the festival, the Greenland women wear their traditional red and white costume.

The Arctic summer

The sun slowly returns. The snow melts, flows away and evaporates. In June, the Arctic summer makes its appearance. All of a sudden, the tundra is covered with a short-lived tapestry of flowers.

It is as if the arrival of summer produced an explosion of joy in the Arctic regions. Nature herself seems to rejoice! The tundra is defined by its permafrost, which means that the soil under the surface is permanently frozen. But the surface melts in summer, creating shallow marshland. The frozen ground melts and suddenly returns to life. It shelters a million sleeping seeds that seek new life. In a matter of a few weeks, there is astounding growth, fuelled by the almost continuous sunlight of the midnight sun. Many plants flower: the yellow and the white poppy, the red willow, the mauve willow-herb. Some of these are useful: the shaggy head of cotton grass served in the past to line Inuit boots. Bilberry and other berries abound, as do fungi such as the edible boletus.

Animals too take advantage of the summery conditions. Migrating birds, which spend the winter in the warm south, return to the Arctic. Terns and auks make their nests. The rich insect life of summer provides food for the nestlings. Swarms of mosquitoes are everywhere and can drive the reindeer mad!

The flowers of the polar regions, the Lapland cassiope and the downy willow, are small and sturdy.

A herd of musk oxen

The wild, shaggy musk oxen wander in serried ranks through the Arctic tundra. Here they are seen in the Taymyr Peninsula.

Squat and short-legged, buried in its mass of hair, the musk ox is designed for the Arctic Circle, where it lives in herds. It is a ruminant, like the reindeer, and loves to graze the tundra. It scratches the snow with its broad hooves to uncover the lichens and mosses that it feeds on. Males can weigh up to 350 kilograms and have a profound sense of community. To defend themselves against wolves, their main predator, they form a circle, in the centre of which they place females and young. Then they confront the enemy with their long, sharp horns. Males also fight one another for females during the rutting season in late summer. They then give off a very powerful scent called 'musk', which gives them their name and is intended to attract the female musk ox.

The fleece of the musk ox is like a wonderfully thick, dense pullover that keeps body-heat in. But it is not very good against rain; the soaked hairs freeze when the cold returns and the animal can die of hypothermia.

The virtues of musk-ox fur (the warmest in the world, with individual hairs up to ninety centimetres long) attracted trappers and the animal was hunted to the brink of extinction. It is now protected. It lives free in Alaska and Canada, in particular on Banks Island, which has 68,000 of them. It was reintroduced into Siberia in 1970.

Musk oxen renew their coat every year.
This is the moulting season.

Pacifying the evil spirits

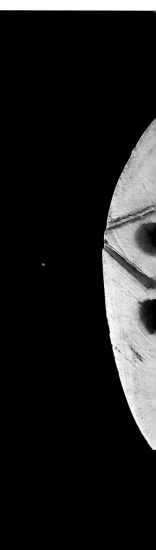

The Arcti peoples believe that jewels and amulets will protect them against evil spirits. The Dolgans of Siberia use mammoth-ivory, making the amulets even more valuable!

Throughout the Arctic region, the shaman is greatly respected. He is the religious chief of a clan or village. The Dolgans, like the Inuits and the Sámi, are animists who believe that nature is inhabited by spirits. They are particularly afraid of the hidden spirits that haunt the tundra and the glaciers, believing that only the shaman can communicate with these all-powerful beings. Cajoling the spirits with offerings, the shaman cures illnesses by magic and wards off the spells that threaten the shepherd and his reindeer herd.

To avert these evil spells, animists perform many different kinds of ritual. For example, the Dolgans always walk around a sacred site in a particular direction (clockwise or anti-clockwise). They avoid coming close to a rock under which an evil spirit might be sleeping. They also invoke the spirit of fire, asking him to keep their goods safe—and first and foremost their little house on runners, the *balok*.

The Dolgans also wear amulets. In the Taymyr Peninsula of Siberia, these little objects, a kind of good-luck charm, are sculpted in mammoth ivory, the only valuable material found in the region. Mammoths were a kind of prehistoric elephant. When they died, their bodies were preserved by the cold and remained buried in the tundra as if in a freezer. From time to time, the Dolgans unearth a mammoth bone or tusk and put it to use.

The Dolgans organise shamanic ceremonies to drive out evil spirits.

A mammoth called 'Jarkov'

With the exception of his impressive tusks, this very old mammoth is completely concealed inside this block of ice. He died some 20,000 years ago and his body has been preserved intact by the extreme cold of Siberia.

The story of this extraordinary scientific discovery begins in December 1997. Bernard Buigues, a French expert on fossils (paleontologist), was working in the Taymyr Peninsula. One morning, he tripped over a big piece of bone in the frozen tundra. At first, he had no idea that it could be a mammoth. But the Dolgans, who know that such frozen beasts occasionally turn up in this region, were quick to show him another site nearby, where a pair of tusks some three metres long was sticking up!

Money had to found for the *Mammuthus* expedition and in September 1999, a team of scientists set up a base in Khatanga, the main town of the region. With the temperature at –40° Celsius, it took five weeks to cut open the earth around the frozen mammoth with pneumatic drills. Finally, on October 17, 1999, the mastodon, still in its enormous block of ice, was winched up by a very powerful helicopter. It was transported to Khatanga and there a special underground laboratory with a constant temperature of –15° Celsius was built to hold it. Scientists can now study it without it decomposing (rotting away).

The mammoth has been dubbed 'Jarkov' after the surname of the Dolgan who found it. Having examined it, the scientists conclude that Jarkov died at the age of forty-seven, a mere 20,380 years ago.

Jarkov was surrounded by a twenty-ton block of ice. He himself weighs three tons!

Scientific expeditions

A few tents standing in the vast white plains of the Taymyr Peninsula are the outward sign of a major scientific campaign to understand the mysteries of the Arctic region.

The Arctic glaciers and the frozen subsoil of the tundra afford new perspectives for contemporary science. They were formed tens of millions of years ago and the cold has conserved rare traces of that remote past. They are therefore like a time-machine, allowing us access to prehistory. Core samples taken by drilling down into the depths of the *Inlandis* in Greenland offer cylindrical cross-sections of this past and help scientists understand aspects of prehistory such as climate.

Many countries take part in this research. And this international cooperation is nothing new. It began with the International Polar Year (IPY), a programme of research into the Polar regions, in 1882–3. There was a second IPY in 1932–3 and a third in 1957–8. The next is scheduled for 2007–8. Presided over by the United Nations Educational Scientific and Cultural Organisation (UNESCO), it will bring together scientists from more than thirty countries. Their goal is to understand the role of the Polar climate in regulating the climate of the rest of the world and to evaluate the threat of global warming.

Warmly wrapped up though they are, the scientists cannot avoid ice forming on their moustaches.

Heat wave in the Arctic

These metal works in Norilsk in northern Russia are representative of the contribution made by industry to global warming. Moreover, their toxic fumes are serious pollutants and the Arctic is suffering.

After much calculation, scientists have come to the conclusion that earth's climate is warming and that much of this warming is due to the carbon-dioxyde (CO_2) emitted by cars, planes and industry. What is more, these effects are twice as clear at the two poles than anywhere else on the planet. Figures published in 2004 by the Arctic Climate Impact Assessment (ACIA), an American research institute, show that temperatures have increased by an average of 2° Celsius in Alaska and Siberia over the last fifty years. Over the same period, the Arctic ice-shelf has diminished by more than six per cent in area and forty per cent in depth.

Greenland's *Inlandis* has also begun to melt. Elsewhere the frozen subsoil is beginning to melt. The thawing of the subsoil might produce a catastrophe by releasing methane gas till now held captive by the permafrost. Methane or marsh gas, which is produced underground by the rotting of plant matter, is itself an agent in the process of global warming. It might establish a vicious circle; methane release would accelerate global warming, releasing more and more methane. The celebrated astrophysicist, Hubert Reeves, calls this process 'a sleeping dragon' that we should take care not to wake.

Not all pollution is airborne. An oil-tanker pollutes everything around it when it runs aground.

The threat to animal life

This handsome bear, sculpted in ice, is doomed to disappear. Global warming will melt it. And if the ice-shelf can no longer form because of increasing temperatures, the polar bear too will disappear.

The animals of the Arctic are unprepared for global warming, which destroys their ways of life. Polar bears are among the first victims. If the ice-shelf contracts, so do their food supplies. By devouring the seals that they find on the ice between November and May, they build up stocks of fat that allow them to survive the summer months, when they can find little to eat.

With their winter feeding-season at risk, polar bears are living on borrowed time. According to the Canadian Wildlife Service, the 12,000 bears recorded west of Hudson Bay are already showing signs of fragility. Undernourished females are too weak to have offspring or to feed their cubs properly if any are born. Bear birth rates are falling and the scrawny cubs are fifteen per cent below their expected weight. If nothing is done, extinction is inevitable in the long or short term.

The reindeer of the tundra are not much better off. The herds suffer from an indirect consequence of global warming: ice. The subsoil thaws at 0° Celsius but quickly freezes over again when the temperature falls. But the ice formed after the thaw is much harder than snow and the reindeer are not strong enough to break it with their hooves in order to reach their food. The reindeer are dying and the size of the herds is gradually falling.

Famished polar bears sometimes scavenge from dustbins in the hope of finding food.

The polar world adrift

Will these ice floes adrift on the Arctic Ocean disappear as a result of global warming? That would mean the end of the polar region as we know it—and would have alarming consequences for the rest of the world.

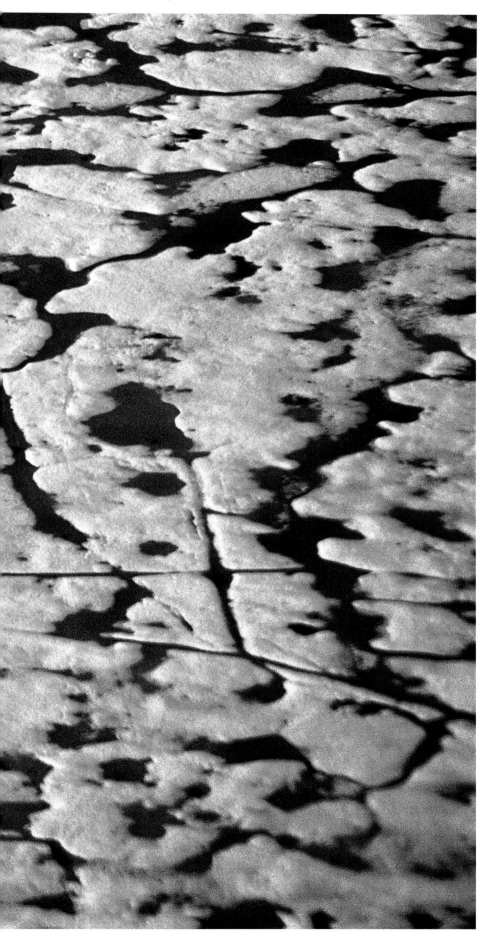

If the ice-shelf of the North Pole and the *Inlandis* of Greenland were both to melt, the sea-level would rise by seven metres throughout the world. Entire countries that now lie just above sea-level, such as Bangladesh and the Maldive Islands in Asia, would be overrun by the ocean.

Fortunately, this is still a distant prospect. But ecologists and scientists are very worried about the thaw that has begun in the Arctic ice sheets. The freshwater liberated by this thaw flows into the oceans and modifies their salinity (the amount of salt in sea-water). This change is already disturbing the life-cycle of certain fishes such as cod, which are becoming rarer.

The change would also affect the Gulf Stream, the warm ocean current to which Western Europe owes its temperate climate. The Gulf Stream flows where it does because of a combination of water temperature and salinity. If the balance were altered, it might have important consequences, altering the flow of the Stream. For the time being, no one can say what these would be. But they might mean that Great Britain and the Atlantic Coast of Europe would undergo further climate change, with very hot summers and very cold winters.

Greenlanders like to melt and drink the very pure water of which the *Inlandis* is made up.

The future of the Great North